PROFILES

GW01402852

Prince

Alan Hamilton

Illustrated by
Nicholas Day

Hamish Hamilton
London

Titles in the Profiles *series*

HAMISH HAMILTON CHILDREN'S BOOKS

Penguin Books Ltd, 27 Wrights Lane, London W8 5TZ (Publishing & Editorial)
and Harmondsworth, Middlesex, England (Distribution & Warehouse)
Viking Penguin Inc., 40 West 23rd Street, New York, New York 10010, U.S.A.
Penguin Books Australia Ltd, Ringwood, Victoria, Australia
Penguin Books Canada Limited, 2801 John Street, Markham, Ontario, Canada L3R 1B4
Penguin Books (N.Z.) Ltd, 182—190 Wairau Road, Auckland 10, New Zealand

First published in Great Britain 1984 by
Hamish Hamilton Children's Books

Copyright © 1984 text by Alan Hamilton
Copyright © 1984 illustrations by Nicholas Day

Reprinted 1987

British Library Cataloguing-in-Publication Data:

Hamilton, Alan, *1943—*
Prince Philip. — (Profiles)
1. Philip, *Prince consort of Elizabeth II Queen
of Great Britain.*　　2. Great Britain—Princes
and princesses—Biography
I. Title　　II. Series
941.085'92'4　　DA591.A2

ISBN 0-241-11167-6

Typeset by Pioneer
Printed in Great Britain at the
University Press, Cambridge

Contents

1 Husband of a Queen

It is not an easy thing for a man to be the husband of a queen, yet not be king himself. Prince Philip, Duke of Edinburgh, is married to Elizabeth the Second, Queen of Great Britain and Northern Ireland, and of sixteen other countries large and small around the world. She is head of the Commonwealth, Queen of more lands and people than any other monarch living, the latest in the longest line of kings and queens still reigning anywhere, and probably the best-known woman in the world.

Prince Philip, on the other hand, may be one of the best-known men in the world, but he is not the head of any country, nor king of anywhere. Prime Ministers do not have to consult him for advice, nor tell him what they are doing, as they must do of the Queen. He does not have to see or sign the important papers of State, as the Queen does. He does not open Parliament, nor review the Trooping the Colour, although he may often be at his wife's side.

If the Queen should die, her eldest son becomes the next monarch. If her husband should die, she carries on being Queen just as before. Prince Philip's only official position is to be a husband and a father, and had he not married the woman who was to become Queen of Great Britain, it is quite likely that very few people would ever have heard of him.

Kings and queens ascend their thrones because their parents sat on thrones. In Britain it has always been much easier for a boy than for a girl. The tradition is that the last monarch's eldest son becomes the next king. Even if the eldest son has a big sister, she will not become queen. The only way that a girl can become queen is if there are no boys. Elizabeth the Second became Queen because her father, King George the Sixth, had only two daughters and no sons. She is Queen Regnant, which means she is Queen in her own right and not just because she is married to a king, which of course she is not.

Almost every day of her life the Queen has to read the official Government papers, which are brought to her twice a day in red leather boxes, and which tell her everything that is going on in the world. Every Tuesday the Prime Minister comes to see her to tell her what the Government is doing. It is the job of a Queen to be told what is going on and to give advice. Prince Philip has no part in that job.

But of course there is more to being Queen than that. The monarch is always being invited to visit places, to attend functions, to open things, to meet people. It is the less official part of her job, but it is still important that she meets people, and is seen by as many of her subjects as possible.

Naturally the monarch receives far more invitations to open town halls and hospitals, to be president of charities and colonel-in-chief of regiments, to visit schools, factories, old people's homes, than she could ever possibly cope with. This is where her husband can shoulder a share of the job, by taking her place and representing the Royal Family at a great many functions where a Royal presence would be considered a great honour.

Most members of the Royal Family take their share of attending functions, and Prince Philip is no exception. And, as we shall see, he has particular subjects in which he is interested.

But a family, even a Royal Family, needs a father, and Prince Philip's most important job of all has been to give the Queen support and encouragement in her work, and to bring up their four children. And although he is not king, he has created for himself a life which is even busier than that of the Queen herself.

2　The Unknown Prince

When it was announced in 1947 that Princess Elizabeth, the future Queen of Britain, was to marry someone called Prince Philip of Greece, people asked: 'Who is this foreign prince? We've never heard of him.'

They were afraid that he might not have enough royal blood in his veins to marry a princess who is a direct descendant of the kings and queens of England reaching back nearly a thousand years to William the Conqueror. As it happened they need not have worried, for if we begin to trace Prince Philip's family tree we soon enter a whole forest of Royal ancestors, and the chief of these is none other than Queen Victoria.

Although she was born at Kensington Palace in London, many of Victoria's close relations were German, and so too were many of her ancestors. Victoria herself, who married a German, had nine children; and when they grew up, many of them went off and married yet more German princes and princesses. In those days it was thought proper that Royals should marry only other Royals, so that their children would be sure of coming from very Royal parents indeed. And so all the Royal families of Europe kept marrying each other.

At the beginning of the twentieth century every country in Europe except France and Switzerland was ruled by a Royal family, and they were almost all related to each other, and to Queen Victoria.

Victoria's eldest son, according to the old custom, followed her as King Edward the Seventh; Edward's son followed him as King George the Fifth; George's son became King George the Sixth; and George the Sixth's eldest daughter followed him as Queen Elizabeth the Second. So the present Queen is, in a perfectly straight line, Victoria's great-great-granddaughter.

Among Victoria's children was a daughter called Princess Alice, who went off and married one of those innumerable German princes, Louis of Hesse. Now Louis and Alice had two daughters, one of whom married the Prince (or Tsar) of Russia and the other of whom married yet another German prince, Louis of Battenberg.

Now this Louis and his new wife (who was also called Victoria) had a daughter called Princess Alice, who in time went off and married another prince. And the prince she found was called Andrew of Greece.

Well, he was called Andrew of Greece, but you will not be surprised to learn that he was really German. His father was King of Greece, but his ancestors, one of whom had become King of Denmark, were from Germany. Prince Andrew's great-grandfather had the terrible name of Duke Frederick William of Schleswig-Holstein-Sonderburg-Glucksburg, although his friends no doubt called him Freddie.

Needless to say, Andrew's mother had German

Princess Alice and Prince Andrew of Greece

connections too. She was Grand Duchess Olga of Prussia, the most powerful of the German states, and her grandfather had been Nicholas the First, one of the most famous Russian Tsars.

Once Andrew and his new wife Alice had sorted out who their ancestors were — which must have taken them a very long time indeed — they went on to have four daughters and one son, and the son was called Philip. He was born on 10 June 1921, on the dining-room table of his parents' house on the Greek island of Corfu.

Many years later, when he was about to marry Princess Elizabeth of Great Britain, he was able to show just how much Royal blood he had in his veins. He and Elizabeth, being both descended from Queen Victoria, were in fact third cousins.

The days when almost every country in Europe had its Royal Family are long gone. Two world wars have changed the map out of all recognition, and most countries nowadays elect their head of state from among politicians. Today there are only ten Royal families left on their thrones in Europe, and none of them is in Germany.

3   Into Exile

Prince Andrew of Greece was a tall, good-looking man
with very blond hair which made him look like a
Viking, and very bad eyesight which forced him to
wear a monocle. He was an officer in the Greek army,
because that is what princes always did if they did not
have a throne.

Shortly after his son Philip was born, Prince Andrew
left the family home of *Mon Repos,* the villa on the
island of Corfu where he and Princess Alice lived with
their five children and five servants, and went off to
fight the Turks.

Ever since Greece had won its independence from
the Turkish Empire, the Turks and Greeks had never
liked each other very much. Even today they are not
the best of friends, and still argue over who owns the
island of Cyprus. On this occasion the argument was
over Anatolia, a stretch of wild mountainous land
between the two countries which had been awarded to
Greece at the end of the First World War, and which
Turkey now decided she wanted back. The Turks
invaded it with their well-trained and well-equipped
army, and the Greeks were hopelessly defeated.

The Greek politicians were furious at the defeat, and

Prince Philip, aged one

they looked around for someone to blame. Important Army officers were arrested, and Prince Andrew was ordered to appear in Athens, the Greek capital, to explain what went wrong. As soon as he arrived he was arrested and put in prison. The Government told him he would be put on trial for treason because, they said, he had been incompetent in the way he had led his regiment, and had retreated when he should have stayed and fought.

Back at the family home in Corfu, Philip's mother became desperately worried about what might happen to her husband, and to the whole family. She knew that the usual punishment for treason was death. But what was she to do?

She immediately contacted all her many Royal relatives around Europe — and you will remember that she was related in some way to most of the Royal families of the time. Most of them did not want to become involved in anything to do with politics, but her relative King George V of Britain decided that he must try and help. So he sent a spy.

The British agent was called Gerald Talbot, and he slipped into Greece in disguise to see what he could do to save Prince Andrew. Meanwhile King George also sent a British warship, *HMS Calypso*, to lie off Athens as a warning and a threat. Prince Andrew was brought before the court and, although he protested his innocence, was found guilty of treason. The court did not want to believe his explanation that his regiment was so small and so poorly trained and equipped that he could never have fought off a Turkish attack.

Louis of Battenberg, First Sea Lord

The Greek politicians were determined to blame somebody for the disaster of the war, and Prince Andrew was sentenced to death at dawn. Talbot, however, had managed to contact the Greek government, told them that they would be extremely unpopular with their friends the British if they executed the Prince, and said that if they would spare his life Prince Andrew would leave Greece forever and never trouble them again.

The government agreed and, as dawn broke Prince Andrew, instead of being taken to face the firing squad, was led by Talbot to the harbour where they boarded

HMS Calypso and immediately set sail for Corfu to collect the rest of the family. Princess Alice had packed a few essential belongings. She and her children bade a reluctant farewell to their home which, although it had no electricity or hot water, they had loved because it was small, comfortable and beautifully situated on the lovely warm island of Corfu.

There was neither time nor room on the warship to take the family furniture. Prince Philip, still barely a year old, needed somewhere to sleep, and the sailors made him a cot out of an old orange box. In such undignified fashion did the infant Philip sail from his homeland into a very uncertain future.

The problem was, where were the family to go? Although they had relatives in most countries of Europe, they had no particular ties with any of them, and very little money, at least not much for a royal family. The best bet seemed to be London where Philip's grandmother, the Marchioness of Milford Haven, lived in Kensington Palace. Grandmother agreed to harbour the fugitives, at least for a while.

The Marchioness was the widow of Louis of Battenberg, one of those innumerable German princes, who had moved to London at the beginning of the century. He had become a complete English gentleman, and had had a distinguished career in the Royal Navy, ending up as First Sea Lord, the absolute top head man in charge of the entire Navy.

But then the First World War broke out, with Britain and Germany as enemies, and the British did not like the idea of their Navy being run by a man who had

Kensington Palace

been born in Germany. Poor Prince Louis, who was completely devoted to England, was forced to give up his job. The King, feeling sorry for him, made him Marquess of Milford Haven, and Louis changed his name from Battenberg to the much more English-sounding Mountbatten.

Soon Prince Andrew and his family were on the move again. They had been glad of their temporary refuge in Kensington Palace, but they had no real ties with England and, worse, they had very little money. The baby Philip was next moved to Paris to stay with his father's brother Prince George, who set the family up in a comfortable flat.

Here Philip remained until he was old enough to go

to school, and it was to be a very long time before he had another permanent home. He did not even spend much time in Paris, for he was always being packed off on long holidays with his countless Royal relatives around Europe. Sometimes it would be to stay with the King of Romania, sometimes to cousins in the south of France, and sometimes back to England to see his uncles George and Louis, who were the sons of the Marquess of Milford Haven, the Battenberg who became Mountbatten.

The strain of exile, and the likelihood of never seeing Greece again, began to tell on Philip's parents. Prince Andrew and Princess Alice began to drift apart, he to Monte Carlo where little was ever heard of him, and she to found a religious order of nuns, the Christian Sisterhood of Martha and Mary.

After that, Andrew and Alice had very little to do with bringing up their only son, and Philip spent the rest of his young life being raised by various aunts and uncles. Prince Andrew died in Monte Carlo in 1944, penniless, while Princess Alice withdrew into her order of nuns for many years until she died at Buckingham Palace in 1969, a very old lady in a grey nun's habit, rarely seen and largely forgotten.

4   Hard Schooling

From an early age it was clear that Philip was going to look like his father — tall, slim and blond. But at first he did not show his father's kindly temperament. The young Philip was boisterous and belligerent, often frightening other boys, yet anyone whose home life was as unsettled and uncertain as his would probably have grown up in exactly the same way. He was, however, always bright and interested in everything that was going on around him.

When he was five, Philip's relatives gathered together enough money to send him to a little primary school in Paris called The Elms. When, on his first day, the teacher asked for his full name, he answered, 'Just Philip.' But, said the teacher, he must have a surname. 'No, just Philip — of Greece.' The family name of Schleswig-Holstein-Sonderburg-Glucksburg was much too long for any boy of five to get his tongue around.

The two sides of Philip's family argued about where he should go next. Prince Andrew's side wanted him to go to school back in the family home of Germany, while Princess Alice's side thought he would be much happier and better educated at school in England.

England won. Philip was brought to live with his

Uncle George, who had taken over his father's title of Marquis of Milford Haven, at his home at Lynden Manor near Maidenhead in Berkshire. Uncle George Mountbatten and his brother Uncle Louis Mountbatten were both Navy men, and they told the young Philip stirring tales of the great sea battles of the First World War.

Uncle George found Philip a place at his old school, Cheam, where Uncle George's son David was already a pupil, and where Winston Churchill had once been taught. Like Churchill, Philip was not terribly good at his lessons, but he shone at cricket, football and athletics. Most important, he was happy there, and was glad to have a close young companion in his cousin David.

The other side of the family still thought Philip ought to have some schooling in Germany. A new school had been set up in the old monastery of Salem at

Kurt Hahn, the founder of Gordonstoun

Baden in southern Germany. Its director was Kurt Hahn, a brilliant scholar who had helped to work out the peace treaty when Germany was defeated in 1918. Hahn knew that a new Germany would have to be built after the defeat, and his school was intended to be a very exclusive place for training the boys who would become the country's new leaders. It was an extremely strict school: boys were made to do hard and unpleasant tasks, and there was much more emphasis on dangerous physical sports, mountaineering and life-saving, than on lessons. Hahn believed that was the way to build up strong characters.

But there was someone else who had other plans to rebuild Germany to make it rich and strong again. His name was Adolf Hitler.

Hitler became leader of Germany in 1933, the same year that the eleven-year old Philip finished his preparatory schooling at Cheam and travelled to Germany for a spell of hard character-building under Hahn. But by the time Philip arrived at Salem, Hahn had been arrested because he was Jewish, and Hitler despised all Jewish people.

The school was being run by Hitler's Nazi Party. Most of the teachers were members, and the boys had to join the Hitler Youth movement, have compulsory lessons in Nazi ideas, and give the Nazi salute. Philip was excused because he was a foreigner, and he simply laughed at the teachers and other boys when they shot out their hands shouting 'Heil Hitler!'

It was not a good place for the young Philip to be. Very unpleasant things were going on in Germany, and in less than a year he had been taken away from Salem and sent back to England. Meanwhile there had been such an outcry at the arrest of Kurt Hahn, who was famous and admired all over Europe, that Hitler was forced to release him. Hahn immediately made his way to the safety of Scotland.

He was looking for a site to start another school on the same lines as Salem, and he found it at a little place called Gordonstoun on the windy north-east coast of Scotland near the town of Elgin. He still believed that rugged outdoor sports were more important than formal lessons in a classroom for building a boy's character and making him think for himself.

Gordonstoun was the ideal place for such a school: cold and windy, and close to both sea and mountains. When Hahn took in his first thirty boys in 1934, among them was Philip of Greece.

Again, Philip did not particularly shine in the classroom, but he loved the sports and was out-standingly good at most of them. He particularly loved sailing in the chilly waters of the Moray Firth, and quickly learned the skills of navigation and seamanship. He was not quite so thrilled with the ice-cold baths at six o'clock in the morning.

Hahn noticed that although Philip was not out-standing at academic subjects, he was always willing and enthusiastic about everything he did, and tackled any job with great care and attention to detail. In 1938, Philip's last year at school, Hahn made him Guardian, Gordonstoun's name for Head Boy, and in his final school report Hahn wrote: 'Prince Philip is universally

Prince Philip as Macbeth in the school play

trusted, liked and respected. He has the greatest sense of service of all the boys in the school.'

While Philip was at Gordonstoun his Uncle George Mountbatten, who had come to take the place of his father, died at the age of only forty-six, and the role of father-figure was taken over by the next nearest in the family, George's brother Louis Mountbatten, still serving in the Navy. Between them Louis Mountbatten, known to Philip as Uncle Dickie, and Kurt Hahn the headmaster, were probably the two biggest influences in young Philip's life.

5 A Prince at War

Philip left Gordonstoun without any of the qualifications needed to go to college or university, but it did not much matter. There was very little doubt about what he would do next. Because both his English uncles were sailors, and because he had been so proficient in his sailing lessons at school, he was obviously destined for the Royal Navy. Many years later, however, Prince Philip admitted that left to himself he would rather have joined the Royal Air Force.

So early in 1939, at the age of seventeen, Philip went to the Royal Naval College at Dartmouth in Devon, where three English kings — George the Fifth, Edward the Eighth and George the Sixth — had previously trained as naval officers. Philip did not do particularly well in his entrance examinations, coming sixteenth out of thirty-four candidates. But it was good enough to let him in, and he was soon to prove himself one of the brightest students in the college.

That summer King George the Sixth, cruising along the south coast in the old Royal yacht *Victoria and Albert,* paid a visit to his old college and was shown around by his friend Lord Louis Mountbatten. With him the King brought his two daughters, the Princesses Elizabeth and Margaret.

As the girls were not likely to be interested in tagging along behind a couple of old men chattering about ships, and as there was an outbreak of mumps among the college students, it was thought better that the girls be taken to a nearby house and entertained for the afternoon. Mountbatten suggested that one of the students come and look after them, and he called for his nephew Philip.

They played with a model train set, then went outside where Philip showed off by jumping over the tennis nets. The next day, as a reward for looking after the princesses, he was invited to lunch aboard the Royal yacht. When *Victoria and Albert* finally sailed away pursued by a flotilla of small boats, it was Philip in his rowing boat who was the last to turn away and head for home, after the yacht's captain had shouted at him that he was a silly young man for sailing so dangerously close.

At that time Princess Elizabeth was a child of only thirteen, and knew nothing of boys, but that first meeting with Philip was one she would never forget.

On active service in the Second World War

By the time Philip had finished his training as an officer and had passed out of the college with distinction in 1940, Britain was again at war with Germany, fighting the menace of Adolf Hitler. Philip was now ready to join the Royal Navy, but he presented a problem. Strictly speaking he was not British. He was still Greek, and Greece was a neutral country which had not yet joined the war. Besides, some of Philip's relatives were German, some supported Hitler, and at least one had joined the Luftwaffe, the German air force which was soon to bomb Britain.

Philip himself, like his grandfather Prince Louis of Battenberg, had no doubt that he was absolutely pro-British. Some behind the scenes string-pulling by his Uncle Dickie, now in command of his own ship, solved the problem. Philip was posted to *HMS Ramillies*, which was British but well out of the way of the main action, escorting Australian convoys in the Indian Ocean, and therefore not too likely to be shot at.

But this was not good enough for Philip, who did not want to spend the war in a quiet and safe backwater. He complained to Uncle Dickie, who managed to pull a few more strings and have his nephew transferred to a more active ship. What suddenly made it much easier was that Greece, having been invaded by the Italians and Germans, was now in the war on the side of the British.

Soon Philip found himself serving in *HMS Valiant* in the Mediterranean, escorting and defending convoys landing British troops on the Greek island of Crete. For the first time he saw real active service, as his ship was fired on and bombed.

Valiant attacked and sunk two Italian destroyers, and for his part in the action Philip was mentioned in despatches, and the King of Greece awarded him a medal. As a junior officer, Philip gained a reputation among the ship's crew for demanding strict discipline and insisting that everything be done absolutely right. He wanted his ship to be the best and smartest in the flotilla.

Even during wartime, fighting men are occasionally allowed holidays, and on one occasion in 1943 Philip found himself on Christmas leave in England with nowhere to go. He managed to get himself an invitation to Windsor Castle, where the Royal Family had moved during the bombing of London.

Christmas at Windsor became a Royal Family

With Princess Elizabeth outside Windsor Castle

tradition, and their favourite way of entertaining themselves and their guests was to stage pantomimes. Philip watched the young Princess Elizabeth play the principal boy in Aladdin, and nearly fell out of his seat with laughing. It was not long afterwards that a picture of the prince, wearing a beard and full naval uniform, appeared on Princess Elizabeth's dressing table.

As the war progressed Philip made more calls at Windsor whenever he had leave in England. He and Elizabeth got on well together, not least because they were both from the same kind of background, being members of Royal families, and they were bound to have the same interests, and know the same kind of people. People began to whisper that romance might be in the air.

King George the Sixth realized that his elder daughter might well be falling in love with the handsome young naval officer who came to call, and he was worried. As the war came to a close in 1945 Elizabeth was only eighteen and because of the war and her position as the King's daughter, she had never had much chance to meet other young men. Besides the King knew that as he had no sons, Elizabeth would almost certainly become Queen when he died. It was important that she did not rush into marriage with the first young man she had ever known well.

Even when the war was over, and Philip returned with the Navy to a shore job in England with the chance to see Elizabeth much more often, King George said to his daughter what all children hate their fathers to say: 'You must be patient, and wait a while.'

The engagement is announced

6   Royal Wedding

In the summer of 1946 the Royal Family took their usual long holiday at Balmoral Castle in Scotland. They invited Philip to join them. King George and Queen Elizabeth wanted to take a good long look at the young naval lieutenant whom their daughter had so clearly fallen in love with.

Philip, who was still an ordinary and not very senior officer in the Navy, living in a draughty camp in southern England and earning only eleven pounds a week, jumped at the chance. He still had no proper home to go to, and he was delighted to get away from service life for a while and be with Elizabeth. It was there that he asked her to marry him, and she said yes.

King George worried a great deal. He was a possessive father who hated the idea of his beloved daughter leaving home, especially as she was only twenty years old. But there were bigger problems for him to worry about: Philip was Greek, and there were some rather important goings-on in Greece just at that time.

The Greeks had lost their king when their country was invaded during the war. Now that the war was over, there was a furious argument going on about whether they should have a king back again, or whether they should become a republic with a president. The country was on the verge of a civil war. King George did not want to upset the Greeks by announcing that one of their princes was about to join the British Royal Family. It might look as though the Greek Royal Family were abandoning their own country.

So he told Philip and Elizabeth that they could marry, but on condition that they kept their plans absolutely secret until all the problems could be sorted out. And just to make sure, he took Elizabeth off on a long Royal tour of South Africa, to give her the opportunity to change her mind. Changing her mind was the last thing Elizabeth intended to do.

Philip himself was extremely keen to become a British citizen, because being Greek meant that he would never be promoted very far in the Royal Navy, even if his uncle Louis Mountbatten *was* an admiral. Applying meant filling in a long form, convincing the British government that he would be a good and loyal citizen, and paying a fee of ten pounds.

His application was granted. It looked as if Uncle Dickie had been at work behind the scenes again; he was very anxious for his nephew to do well, as though to make up for the misfortune that had befallen his father Louis of Battenberg at the start of the First World War.

Soon afterwards the Greeks made up their minds that they wanted their king back after all, so another obstacle was removed. Finally, as he wanted to marry a woman who would one day become head of the Church

Waving to the crowds after the wedding

of England, he had to change his religion from Greek Orthodox to Anglican; the Archbishop of Canterbury said there would be no difficulty. When Elizabeth returned from South Africa early in 1947, the way was clear for her and Philip to announce their engagement, and the date of their wedding.

The next thing for King George to worry about was what sort of wedding it should be. It was 1947, and Britain was exhausted after the war. Thousands of people were still homeless, the country had just suffered the hardest winter in living memory, and everything was in desperately short supply. Food, clothes, petrol, sweets were all rationed, and all kinds of luxuries, from bananas to motor cars, were almost unobtainable for most ordinary people.

The King thought that, in these hard times, people would be very offended if he gave his daughter an expensive and lavish wedding; a quiet private ceremony would be best. Nonsense, said the Government. What the people really wanted was a splendid and glittering wedding to cheer them up in these hard, drab days. So, on 20 November 1947, a splendid wedding took place in Westminster Abbey. Philip wore his naval uniform and Elizabeth, who was allowed only the same clothes ration as any other girl getting married, still managed to appear in a sparkling dress flowing with pure silk.

Philip and Elizabeth received 2,660 wedding presents, including a grand piano from the air force, a sideboard from the navy, a picnic set from Princess Margaret, and a turkey from a little girl in New York who had heard that the English had nothing to eat.

There was one remaining problem about the marriage, which was that the future Queen could not really become Mrs Schleswig-Holstein-Sonderburg-Glucksburg. Now that he was a British citizen, Philip thought he ought to have an English-sounding surname, having spent his entire life until then without using a surname at all. He considered several, but finally chose that of his English uncle. Prince Philip of Greece gave up his Greek title, and became plain

Lieutenant Philip Mountbatten.

But that was rather too plain for the husband of a future Queen. Shortly before the wedding, King George awarded him the title Duke of Edinburgh, which had last been used by one of Queen Victoria's children, and which was a reminder that his wife would become Queen of Scotland too. Just in case the Welsh felt left out, the King also made him Earl of Merioneth, and to satisfy the English he added the title of Baron Greenwich.

King George also invested both Philip and Elizabeth with the Order of the Garter, the highest order of chivalry in England. But Elizabeth was given hers eight days before Philip, a small reminder that it was she, and not her husband, who would one day be the most important person in the land.

7 A Home of his Own

Marrying Princess Elizabeth brought the biggest change in Philip's life he had ever known. It was a change he thought was mostly good, but it brought its own problems and difficulties.

The best part was that, for the first time since he had been a tiny baby in Corfu, he had a proper home of his own. Soon after their wedding, and their honeymoon spent at Louis Mountbatten's home in Hampshire and at Birkhall, a country house near Balmoral, the couple moved into Clarence House, a Royal residence near Buckingham Palace. The house needed major repairs after wartime damage, and Philip took a great interest in what the architects and builders were doing, often making suggestions of his own about how the work should be done.

The architects and builders were surprised at his interest, and not always terribly pleased. Never before had they come across a member of the Royal Family with such strong ideas about what they should be doing. But Philip was determined that his first proper home should be just how he wanted it.

He was soon to discover the difficult side of his new life. Having joined the Royal Family, he was expected to take part in public duties, and accompany Princess Elizabeth when she attended official functions. He went with his wife to Paris in 1948 to open an exhibition of British life, and learned very quickly that being a Royal meant that public duties must always be carried out, and that when he was on public view he was never allowed to be bored, or tired, or unwell.

Attending functions with his wife meant that Philip had to give up most of his spare time (he was still an officer in the Navy, which he enjoyed most of all). He was keen for promotion, and soon after his marriage he was posted to a course at the Royal Naval College at Greenwich, and this meant he could come home to his new wife and house only at weekends.

Still, it was the period in Philip and Elizabeth's life when they came closest to living the lives of ordinary people. In 1948 their first son was born, and christened Charles Philip Arthur George. It gave Philip great pleasure to know that this son of his would probably be King of Great Britain one day, and it gave even greater pleasure to Louis Mountbatten, who had always been anxious to have his family's good name restored, and who in later years was to grow very attached to Charles as he grew up.

Soon afterwards the Navy sent Philip to Malta to take command of a ship, *HMS Magpie,* which he ran on strict lines and made his crew work very hard. He still wanted his ship to be the smartest in the fleet, and he would not stand for any laziness or slapdash work. Elizabeth paid long visits to Philip in Malta, and although crowds tended to gather wherever they went, and local bigwigs insisted on staging grand balls in their honour, the couple managed to have a reasonably quiet and ordinary life. In his spare moments, Philip was taught to play polo by his Uncle Dickie.

But all the time Philip knew that the Navy career he enjoyed so much could come to an end at any moment, and it worried him a great deal.

Philip had always been aware that his wife would one day become Queen because her father, King George the Sixth, had no sons. But he did not expect that to happen for a very long time. When he married Elizabeth, the King was only fifty-two years old, and Philip looked forward to many years of normal life as a Navy officer before being forced to take up the position of husband to a Queen.

But it was not to be. King George had never been a very strong man, and the effort of leading his country through the years of war had exhausted him. Not long after the wedding, the King became ill, and although he recovered he was never quite the same man again. He began to be ill more and more frequently, and it became gradually more difficult for him to carry out his job as monarch. That meant he had to hand over much of his work to his daughter, who became quite used to carrying out the visits and functions that her father was too ill to undertake.

In 1951 Philip was given leave from the Navy to return from Malta to help his wife with her ever-increasing burden of Royal duties. He knew, secretly, that he would never return to the Navy again, and he was a very disappointed man. Even though he was glad

On their honeymoon at Broadlands, Hampshire

to be back in his home at Clarence House with his son and his newly-born daughter Anne, it was still hard for him to come to terms with having to give up the career at sea he so enjoyed.

But he had no choice, and there was nothing for it but to make the best of his new-found situation, even though he went through spells of deep gloom. To take his mind off the sea and to help his wife with her mounting burden of official tasks, Philip took on some Royal duties of his own.

He already had some experience. Soon after his marriage he had agreed to become president of the National Playing Fields Association after touring bomb-damaged areas of east London and seeing that the children had no proper places to play. Royals often lent their names to worthy organizations, but until now they rarely took an active part in their work, apart from attending the occasional meeting or charity ball. This was not good enough for Philip. If he was to be someone's president, he wanted a say in what they were doing. Otherwise he felt he would be wasting his time and theirs. He launched a £500,000 appeal for the playing fields, and largely because of his fund-raising efforts the Association was soon opening 200 new playing fields every year.

Back in London in 1951 he agreed to become president for the year of another important body, the British Association for the Advancement of Science. This meant making a speech at their conference in Edinburgh. Traditionally, when members of the Royal Family made speeches, they always took care to sound

Proud parents with their first son, Prince Charles

important but actually to say nothing of any importance at all. They were never supposed to offend anybody. But this was not Philip's style. He was only a lieutenant in the Navy, but in his speech he told the scientists in no uncertain terms that industry was being very slow in using new scientific discoveries, and it was high time they did something about it. All the old fuddy-duddies were astonished that a Royal had said something controversial. In fact he had not said anything wildly exciting, but because it came from the lips of a Royal people sat up and took notice. And it was such a welcome change from the dull, boring speeches that Royals usually made at public functions.

Meanwhile the King's health was failing. He had planned to make a major Royal tour of Africa, Australia and New Zealand, to thank the people of the Commonwealth for their help in the war. But he was too ill, and it was decided that Elizabeth and Philip should go in his place. The King waved them off from Heathrow Airport on a wet and windy day on 31 January 1952. They never saw him again.

Less than a week later Elizabeth and Philip were visiting a game reserve in Kenya; they had been up most of the night watching elephants drinking at a water hole. Early the next day one of Philip's staff, who had had a telephone call from London, brought him the news that King George the Sixth had died in his sleep at Sandringham in Norfolk, in the same house in which he was born.

Philip sought out his wife and quietly told her that she was no longer Princess Elizabeth — she was Queen. Within an hour the Royal party had packed their bags and were on their way back to London to a new and very different life.

8　First Man, Second Citizen

Philip's wife, who had left England little more than a week before as Princess Elizabeth, Duchess of Edinburgh, now returned as Queen Elizabeth the Second. Philip remained Duke of Edinburgh, but almost everything else about his life changed.

First, the Royal couple had to leave Clarence House, of which Philip had grown so fond, and move back into the huge draughty rooms and endless long corridors of Buckingham Palace. Elizabeth was more used to it than Philip, for she had lived there until her marriage, but Philip found it a cold, lonely place.

Second, although the Queen by virtue of her marriage to Philip was Mrs Mountbatten, she decided on ascending the throne that she and her children would take her father's name of Windsor. This was the name for the Royal Family chosen by the Queen's grandfather, King George the Fifth. He, like Philip, had a German name — in George's case it was Saxe-Coburg-Gotha, inherited from Prince Albert — and, like Philip, thought it would be much better to have an English one.

One day, Philip's name will be restored to the Royal Family because the Queen has since decided that those

The coronation

of her descendants who are not princes or princesses, and who need a surname, will be called Mountbatten-Windsor. So a grandchild of Prince Andrew or Prince Edward might well be called Lord Philip Mountbatten-Windsor, or Lady Elizabeth Mountbatten-Windsor.

Third, Philip suddenly found that he had to take second place to his wife. He was head of the family and father of their children, but she was Queen. To make sure he had plenty to do, and to make use of his great talent for organizing things, Elizabeth put him in charge of the arrangements for her coronation.

It was a glittering occasion, at a time when Britain was just beginning to recover from the terrible effects of the war — the rationing of food, sweets and petrol was ending, new houses were being built for people made homeless by the bombing, and the whole country was looking forward to a brighter future. The crowning of a new Queen seemed to herald the coming of a new, better age.

The only thing that went wrong with the coronation was the weather. The forecasters had said that the one day in the year most likely to be sunny was 2 June, so that was the day chosen for the ceremony. It rained, in fact it poured, but Philip could hardly be blamed for that. Inside Westminster Abbey, in the first coronation in history to be seen live on television, Philip was the first of the lords and nobles to kiss the new Queen's hand and swear allegiance to her.

It was a symbolic gesture, showing to the whole world that Philip was not King, merely the husband of a Queen. The big question now was what exactly his job was, for there are no easy textbooks which explain what a Queen's husband should do.

For the Queen, there was no doubt about what her duties were. Every day, twice a day, for the rest of her reign, she would have to read the State papers which came to her morning and afternoon in red leather-covered boxes, and told her everything the Government was doing, and everything about the world contained in secret messages sent home from British ambassadors around the world. Every Tuesday evening she would have to see her Prime Minister to be kept up to date on the Government's plans. And she would have to hold countless audiences and investitures, sign endless papers, and attend all manner of official engagements. Such is the work of a monarch.

Things had changed since the time of Prince Albert, who was the last Queen's husband without being King. Queen Victoria was extremely fond of her husband,

The Queen and Prince Philip on tour

and leant on him a great deal for advice, even showing him the daily boxes of secret papers and asking him what he thought the Government should be doing. The Government of the time did not like that at all. They did not think the Queen should tell her husband all the State secrets, especially as he was a foreigner. But when Victoria came to the throne she was very young and inexperienced, and she needed Albert's help and support in her duties.

By the time Elizabeth came to the throne, everyone knew much more clearly exactly what the monarch's job should be, and it certainly did not include sharing her work with her husband, especially as he too was a foreigner by birth. But Elizabeth was better prepared than Victoria had been for becoming Queen. Her father had been very careful to train her in all the duties of a monarch, because he had always known that his daughter would one day have to take over from him.

So Philip was really shut out from the official part of his wife's life, except of course when she went on important visits and Royal tours, when he was naturally expected to accompany her. Soon after the coronation the Queen and the Duke set out on the longest Royal tour that any monarch had ever undertaken, circling the world in 173 days.

Such things had suddenly become possible, because Elizabeth had come to the throne at the dawn of the age of jet aircraft. Since then she has become the most far-travelled monarch of any country in history, and wherever she has gone Philip has usually been by her side.

From the beginning of her reign Queen Elizabeth took her duties very seriously indeed. She knew that less than twenty years before the monarchy had gone through a very bad patch when her father's elder brother, King Edward the Eighth, had given up the throne to marry a divorced woman. Kings were not supposed to do that sort of thing, and both King George and his daughter worked hard to ensure that people believed once more that having a monarch was a good thing.

Because she worked so hard, Elizabeth needed the support of her husband, even though she did not share her official work with him. She needed him at home to be a firm and attentive father to their children, and it was Philip who was in charge there. He sent Prince Charles to his old preparatory school at Cheam, and all three of his sons have followed him to the school he enjoyed so much, Gordonstoun.

But just being a husband and a father was not enough for Philip, who has enormous energy and a great desire to be up and doing things. He needed a job, and because there was no-one to tell him what he should do, and no-one since Queen Victoria's time who had been in his situation, he had to invent a job all by himself.

9 A Life of his Own

There is a tribe of primitive people on a remote island of the New Hebrides in the South Pacific on the other side of the world who worship photographs of Philip and believe that one day he will arrive among them and save them, as though he were God.

He is, of course, just an ordinary man, but he has tremendous energy and never likes to waste a minute of his life. The job that he has created for himself means that he works much harder than most men, and much harder even than the Queen, although he has no official position in the monarchy. Only on the Royal Family's long holidays in the summer and at Christmas does he really relax.

Soon after she came to the throne the Queen put Philip, with his great talent for organising people and getting things done, in charge of the Royal estates at Windsor and Sandringham. His job was to cut out waste and make them work more efficiently. But he realised he could do much more than that.

Because he had no official position, he could move around the country much more easily, and meet many more people informally than the Queen ever could. So he decided that he would become the eyes and ears of

Prince Philip today

the monarchy, getting to know as many people in different walks of life as possible so that he could keep the Queen informed on what the country was really doing and thinking.

Being the Queen's husband, he also received hundreds of invitations to become president, or patron, or chairman, of all manner of different organizations. He accepted, and still accepts, only those where he thought he could be of some real help to them, and he turned down those he suspected just wanted to be able to use his name on their notepaper. He also decided at the beginning that he would not stay in any of those posts for too long, in case they came to take him for granted.

Naturally he had to steer clear of any organization that had anything to do with politics, because it is very important for the Royal Family not to be seen to favour one political party over another, and they must not be seen to be interfering directly with Government. The Queen is queen of everybody in the country, even those who want to get rid of her.

Philip has found all kinds of organizations to be president of, from the Automobile Association to the Royal Agricultural Society, from the British Association for the Advancement of Science to the Central Council for Physical Recreation. Bodies that have had him as their president have usually found him taking a very active interest in their affairs, full of suggestions for improvements and with plenty of strong opinions about how they should be run.

His special interests have always been industry and

Prince Philip has always shown a keen interest in technology.
Here he inspects a new soft spacesuit in Houston, America

technology, and how they can be modernized, and his
pet hates have always been waste and inefficiency. His
brisk, no-nonsense approach, which comes from
Gordonstoun and the Navy, has often upset people
who would rather things were left the way they were,
and who accuse Philip of not knowing what he is talking
about.

He is quite proud of never having had any formal
education beyond school and the Navy. His skill is in

learning a little about a lot of things, and learning fast, then trying to apply the common sense of someone who approaches a problem from outside with a fresh eye. And, of course, he knows so many influential people that he can work wonders just by a well-placed letter or telephone call.

Another of his jobs has been to blow away some of the cobwebs from the monarchy itself. He realises that it must move with the times if it is to survive. Early in her reign he persuaded the Queen to drop some of the more old-fashioned customs, like the presentation of debutantes — daughters of families who liked to think of themselves as rich or important, who paraded in front of the Queen and thereby thought they had 'arrived' in society. He taught the Queen to make better and livelier speeches, and encouraged her to let the BBC make a film of the Royal Family's life. He thought the ordinary people who paid taxes to keep the monarchy going ought to know more about what they were getting for their money.

Because of the kind of schooling he had at Gordonstoun, he believes that outdoor activities are good for young people, developing character and leadership. Early in the Queen's reign he established the Duke of Edinburgh's Award Scheme, and since then many thousands of young people who have attained their badges have met the founder at the regular presentations under the chandeliers of Buckingham Palace.

To manage all this vast load of work he has his own staff of secretaries at Buckingham Palace. Twice a year

At an arts and crafts class of the Victoria Boys and Girls Clubs

they hold an important meeting to decide which of the many hundreds of invitations Philip will accept in the coming six months. He weeds them out carefully, favouring the ones that are in his areas of special interest, like industrial design, or technology, or sport, but trying to accept as many as his crowded timetable will allow.

During a single year he will attend several hundred functions, make at least one major speech a week, which he will probably write himself, and travel over 100,000 kilometres, either to functions of his own or accompanying the Queen on her tours.

For all this he gets paid no salary, but receives only his expenses for doing the job and running his office. The expenses are paid by the Government to all the members of the Royal Family who undertake official duties, except Prince Charles who has his own income from the Duchy of Cornwall. The expenses are called the Civil List, and in 1983 the Government paid the Royal Family just over £4 million in this way. Most of it went to pay the wages of staff at Buckingham Palace, from secretaries to cleaners. Prince Philip's own allowance for the year was £179,300. It sounds a great deal, but he cannot regard any of it as pocket money.

10 'Fundungus'

A Sunday newspaper once asked its readers, if Britain ever became a dictatorship, whom they would like to have as their dictator. The most popular choice was Prince Philip.

It showed that, although Philip has not always been popular with everybody because of his tendency to say exactly what he thinks, a great many people appreciate and admire his practical, no-nonsense approach to life. The one thing he hates is meaningless mumbo-jumbo and old-fashioned ritual, and has even invented his own word to describe it: 'fundungus'.

Even if he were asked, it is very unlikely that Philip would want to become dictator of Britain. He has often said privately that if there were ever a revolution in Britain to get rid of the Royal Family, he and the Queen should creep away as quietly as possible and not try to put up a fight. But the fact that the great majority of people in Britain want to keep their Royal Family is at least partly due to the efforts of Philip in making sure that the monarchy stays up-to-date. However dutiful the Queen was, if she began to appear dull and old-fashioned people might begin to say that she no longer served any useful purpose.

Philip's special position in the monarchy was recognised by the Queen soon after she came to the throne when, in 1957, she created her husband a prince of the United Kingdom to add to his title of Duke of Edinburgh. So he can once again call himself Prince Philip — but a British, rather than a Greek, prince.

It has never been easy for him, particularly in the early days of the Queen's reign when Philip was forced to give up his naval career. Only three years after the coronation he went off on a very long trip on his own in the new Royal yacht *Britannia* to the southern hemisphere and the Antarctic. He was supposed to be studying wildlife, but really his purpose was to get back to sea for a little while, and have a rest from the stifling atmosphere of the court.

He was away for so long that people began to wonder if he had had a row with his wife; they even wondered if he might be planning to divorce her. That turned out to be quite untrue, and Philip has in fact provided a stable family life for the Queen and her children for more than 35 years. There were times when she was very glad of it, particularly when her sister, Princess Margaret, went through a long period of unhappiness after being forbidden to marry the man she loved because he had been divorced.

When he was younger Philip crammed as much as he possibly could into his life as though there was not a minute to lose — sailing with his friend Uffa Fox, learning to fly, playing polo and cricket, even going to sea in his last days in the Navy with a great pile of office work from his official duties in London sharing his captain's cabin.

Now that he is over sixty years old he has slowed up a little, but not very much. He had to give up playing polo because he began to suffer from arthritis in his wrists, and his chief sport now is carriage driving, racing teams of horses as though they were pulling a stagecoach. His eyesight, like his father's, is bad, and for many years he has worn contact lenses, but they have never prevented him from doing anything.

People who know him well say he is much happier now than in the earlier years of the Queen's reign. It has not always been the life he would have chosen himself; he would have preferred to be a career Navy or Air Force officer at least until he was into his fifties. But he has made the best of his lot. The baby who was carried into exile from his home in Greece with little money, nowhere to go, and very poor prospects, has played his part to ensure the continuation of the British monarchy.